Private Worlds

A visual catalog of progressive toy designs, 1970-1990

A Birchwood Palace publication
BP011

Copyright © 2022 by Andy Sturdevant
Third printing, October 2023
ISBN 978-1-7324076-5-7

Cover photo of "Birds on a Tree" puzzle by Creative Playthings, Princeton, N.J., licensed under CC BY-SA 3.0.

Introduction facing page photo from the University of North Carolina Sea Grant College Program, 1979. Courtesy of the State Library of North Carolina and North Carolina Digital Heritage Center.

Rear back photo of a public playground in Boston, June 1973, by Ernst Halberstadt (1910-87), through the Environmental Protection Agency's Project DOCUMERICA. Courtesy of the U.S. National Archives.

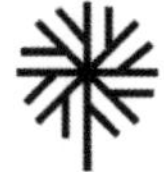

Birchwood Palace Industries, L.L.C. is a publisher of artists books, zines and other small-run printed materials. It is a project of Andy Sturdevant, and is based in Minneapolis, Minnesota. Visit us on the World Wide Web at birchwoodpalace.com

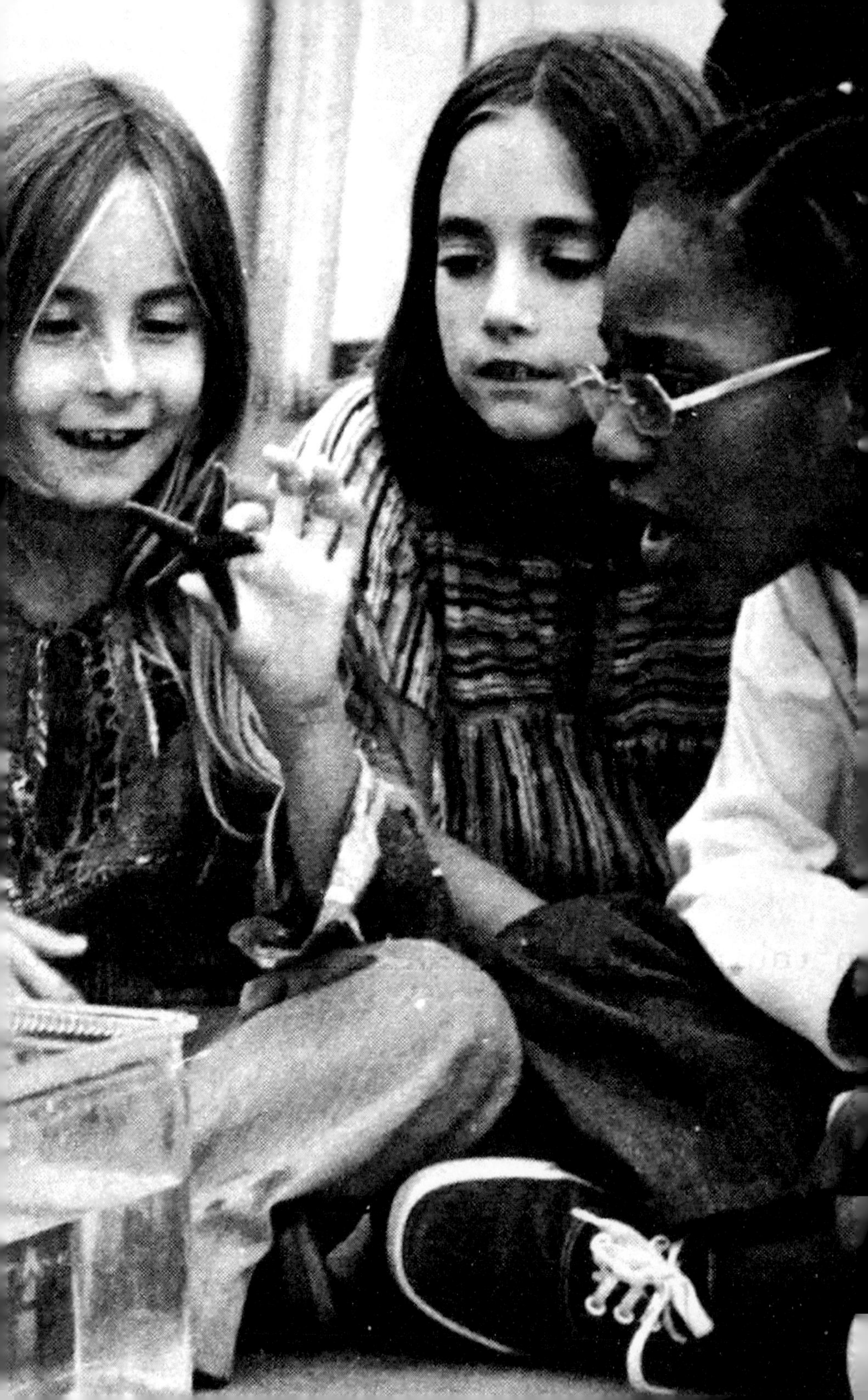

Introduction

"...the pleasure of dwelling in those private worlds is great and irresistible." – Lee M. Rothenberg, U.S. patent application 4,521,203

In early 2022, I became a father for the first time. In the following months, I was brought back into a world I hadn't had anything to do with for decades – the world of children's toys, a $2.5 billion dollar industry domestically, and nearly $95 billion globally. All sorts of wood, rubber, and plastic playthings began to find their way into the house, many of which were unexpectedly delightful for both my son and myself.

The highlights were wood or plastic toys which offered my son several different ways to interact with them, whether through putting them in his mouth and chewing on them, manipulating them, or rolling them around on the floor. Some of these designs seemed vaguely familiar, like they might be at least as old as me. They brought to mind some of my toys from the 1980s. After cleaning up the play area for the night, I'd page through Google Patents on my phone for designs from this period and earlier, curious about the types of familiar and unrealized toys I might find.

The era of my childhood, the 1980s, was a time of intense deregulation for children's television, and to some extent, birthed the worst aspects of consumption-focused contemporary childhood. Following the Federal Communications Commission deregulation by the Reagan administration, the airwaves were flooded with crappy cartoons that were little more than 22-minute advertisements for equally crappy plastic toys. (Crappy cartoons and toys which, it must be said, I adored, though my pacifist mom drew the line at G.I. Joes, who were never deployed to my personal childhood theater of war.)

From the perspective of the 1980s and after, the period right before that seems like a spectacularly imaginative, non-commercial one for children's entertainment and toys. While paging through patent applications of the '70s and '80s, I found a treasure trove of – for lack of a better term – "progressive toys." You may know the kind of toy I mean, especially if you also grew up around a certain type of crunchy boomer parent that dabbled in vegetarianism and *Star Trek*, or let you call them by their first names.

We can look at the toys collected here within their proper historical context and enjoy the eccentric "just tinkering in the garage in the '70s" qualities. Beyond those, however, the best of these toy designs speak to a strain of creativity and idealism that somehow managed to survive the 1980s and continues into this century. They encourage imaginative, unstructured play that helps children to build those private worlds Lee Rothenberg poignantly describes in the epigraph above.

Andy Sturdevant
Summer 2022

Noisemaking Amusement Device

United State Patent 3,837,115
Inventor: Jorma Vennola, Princeton, N.J.
Filed February 22, 1972, granted September 24, 1974

This noisemaker, which resembles a pan flute but works more like a wind chime, was said to make "noises without being unduly loud or disturbing." The child would wave the gum sheet at the corners, and the hollow wooden cylinders would make what is described in the patent application as "a clicking commotion." The device was created by Finnish designer Jorma Vennola (b. 1943) while working as a toy designer in the early 1970s for Creative Playthings, the storied New Jersey educational toy manufacturer. "Play is for anyone, any age, any where," as the company's open-minded credo put it. The Columbia Broadcasting System purchased the company in the 1950s while expanding into the educational market, and Vennola developed a number of patents for them, including several other designs featured in this book. Vennola returned to Finland later that decade, where he went on to create designs for Iittala, the award-winning Finnish modern glassware manufacturer.

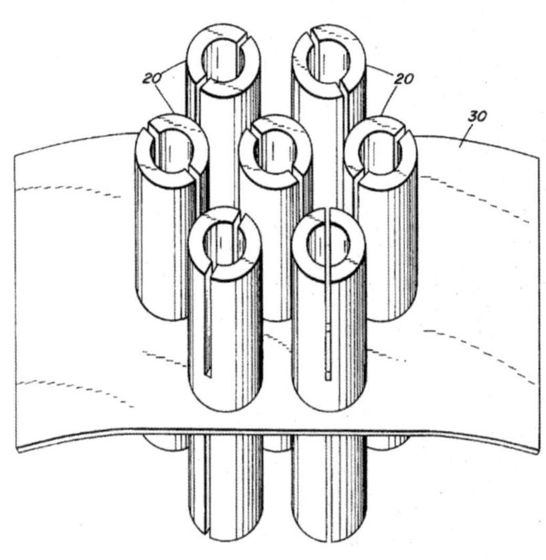

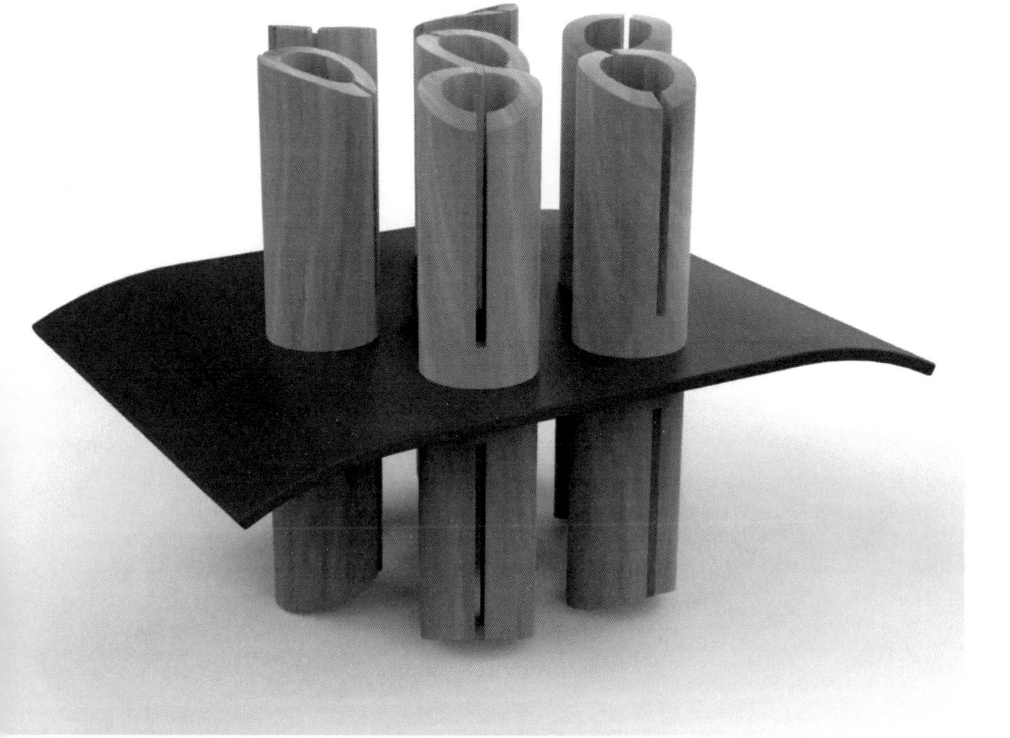

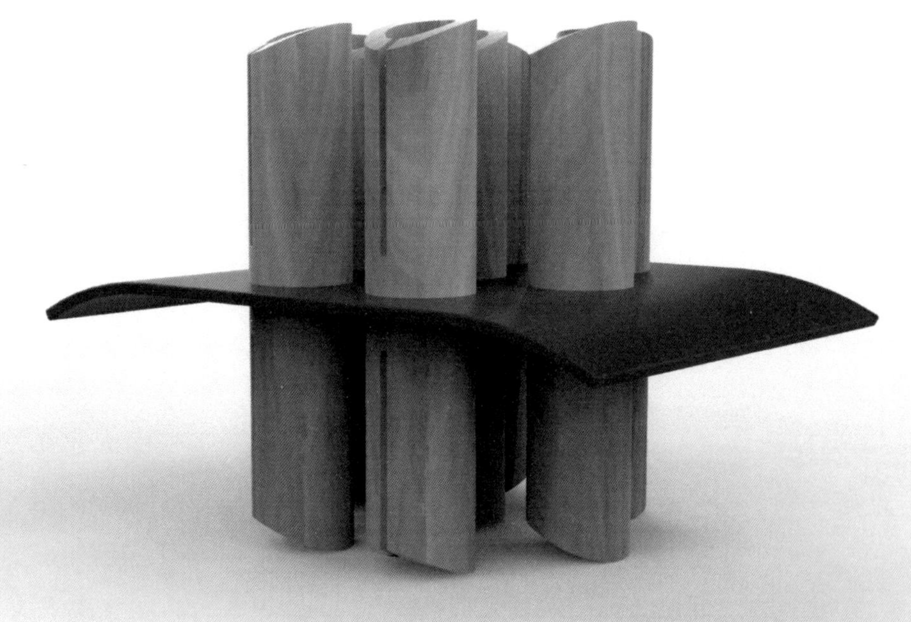

Rolling Toy
Design Serial Number 270,984
Inventor: Jorma Vennola, Princeton, N.J.; and
Erkki-Pekka Korpijaakko, Heightstown, N.J.
Filed July 12, 1972, granted January 15, 1974

The working subtitle for this book was *A Visual
Catalog of Wooden Hippie Toys*, which I might have
ultimately gone with, except that so many of the most
appealing patent designs I found were (1) made with
plastic and not wood and (2) designed by people who
probably did not self-identify as hippies. For example,
the co-creator of this toy, Jorma Vennola, whom we
have already met once and will meet several more
times, was thirty years old, lived in Central Jersey, and
was employed by a subsidiary of one of the largest
mainstream media corporations in America at the time
of the filing. Given these facts, it'd be difficult to desig-
nate him as a "hippie" in any meaningful sense. Sym-
pathetic to the cause? Maybe. Interested in progressive
ideas about children's play? Absolutely. But likely not
out on a commune carving toys out of wood.

That said, most of these items featured in this book
are "wooden hippie toys," at least in spirit if not in
practice. In fact, the undisputed hippie consumer
guide of the age, *The Whole Earth Catalog*, highlight-
ed Creative Playthings as "the old standby for nifty,
new items" in their two-page section on children's toys
in the 1971 edition, along with a few featured toys for
which I sadly could not find patent designs.

This design, by Vennola and his fellow Finnish expat
Korpijaakko, is perhaps the archetypal wooden hippie
toy, and exactly the sort of thing I think of when I
imagine the sorts of objects that phrase conjures
up: open-ended, a little bit noisy, suitable for a wide
age range, imparting a variety of tacticle sensations,
non-representational, and perhaps most importantly,
functional but not practical in any specifically pro-
scribed way. It can be a lot of things – a vehicle, a
magic wand, an instrument, a science fiction device –
but doesn't *have* to be any one of them.

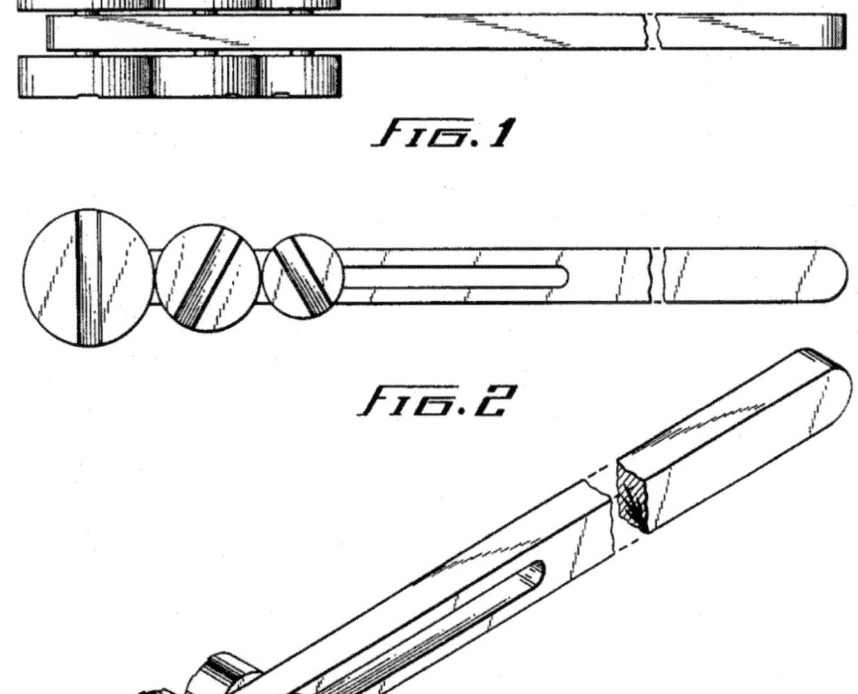

FIG.1

FIG.2

FIG.3

Toy Building Block Suitable for a Pad, Raft or the Like

United States Patent 3,822,499
Inventor: John B. DeVos, Libertyville, Ill.
Filed May 30, 1972, granted July 9, 1974

Though many of these patents were filed on behalf of large corporations, like Creative Playthings and CBS, part of the pleasure of browsing patent applications is seeing the many designs that came from average citizens with no apparent connections or inroads into the toy industry. This design is one such example, filed by John B. DeVos, a dentist in the northern suburbs of Chicago whose only other patent was for a topical cosmetic gel for hardening fingernails and toenails. DeVos' patent application for these polyurethane foam blocks emphasize their lightweight, soft, and durable qualities. Polyeurethane was invented in Germany in the 1930s and was widely used in all industries by the 1950s. In 1969, while looking for a way to design soft toy rocks for a caveman-themed game, a toy developer in Minnesota carved a ball out of polyeurethane to create what would become the first Nerf product. After that, polyeurethane became a staple of toy design. Like Nerf products, these blocks could be easily thrown, assembled, banged around or handled by even very small children, and like all the blocks featured in this book, be used to build elaborate assemblages. Like most if not all the designs in this collection, Dr. De Vos' blocks most likely joined the 95 percent of all patents that are never licensed or commercialized.

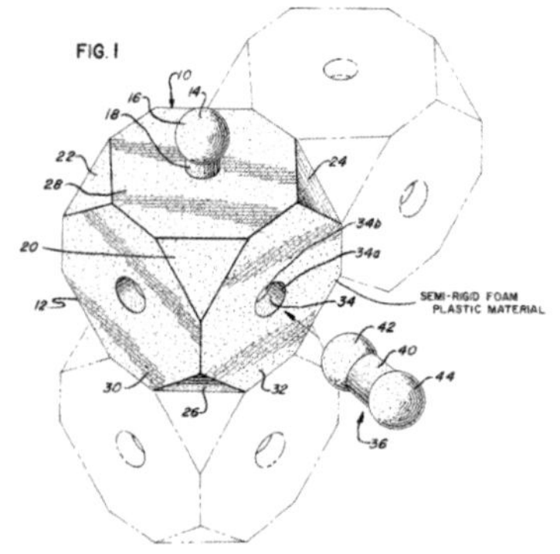

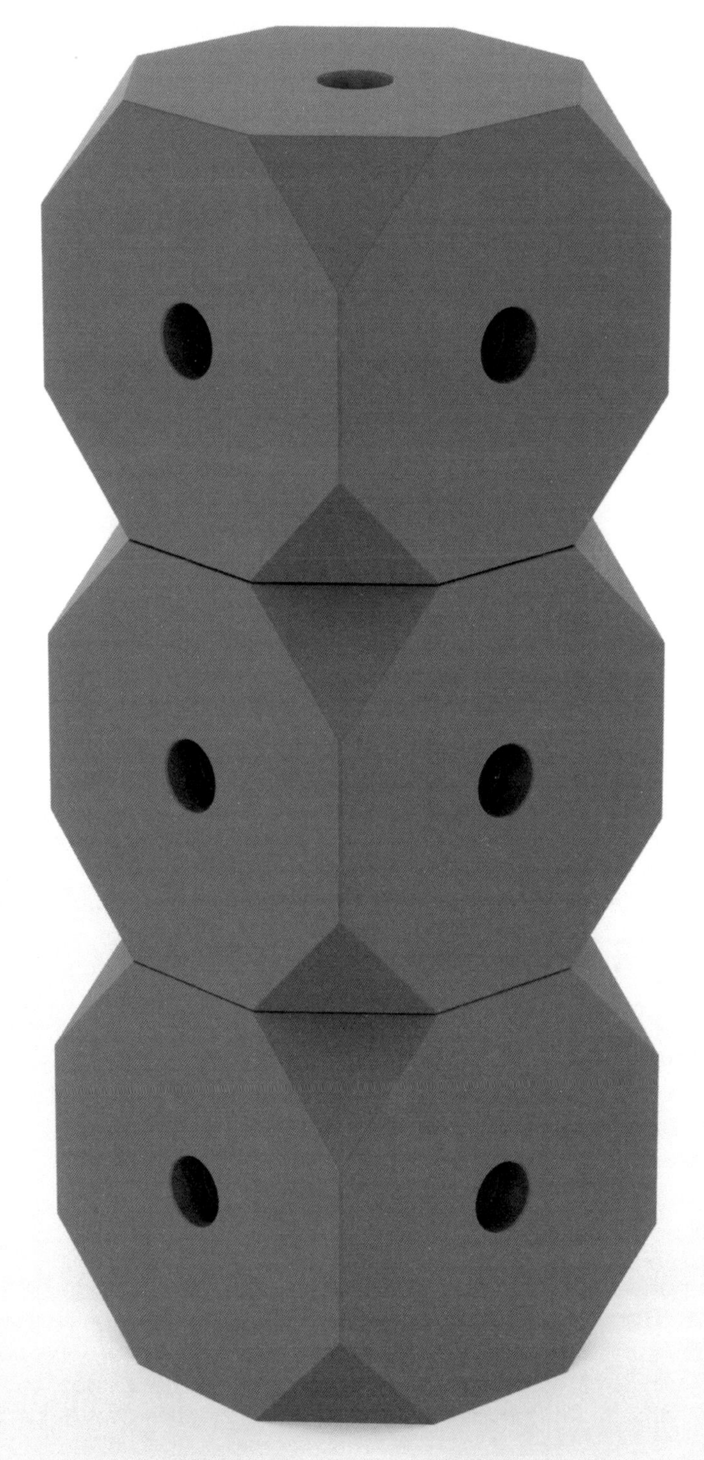

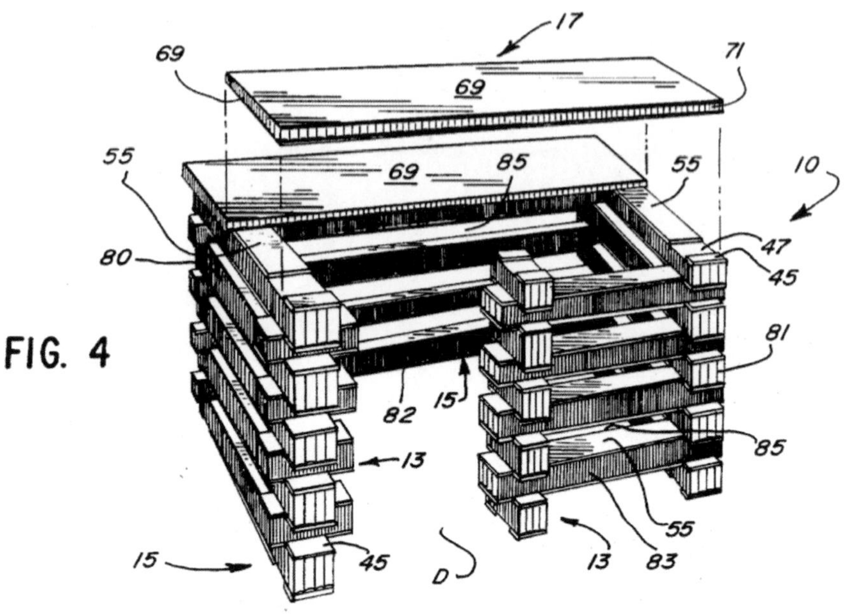

ABOVE: Toy Construction Kit
United States Patent 4,521,203
Inventor: Lee M. Rothenberg, Jr., Homewood, Ill.
Filed April 23, 1984, granted June 4, 1985

A life-size toy construction kit comprising three basic elements: end blocks,
wall logs and enclosure panels, made of honeycomb sandwich kraft board.
Rothenberg filed this application on behalf of the International Honeycomb Corporation of Park Forest, Illinois, a manufacturer of cardboard
packaging who appear to have been taking a shot at the childrens' market.
A poignant turn of phrase in the "Background" section of the application
by Rothenberg, regarding the "private worlds" of children's play, also gives
this book its title.

RIGHT: Interconnecting Building Toy Panels
United States Patent 4,884,988
Inventor: Larry D. McMurray, Seattle, Wash.
Filed October 11, 1988, granted December 5, 1989

These cardboard or plastic panels are assembled with hook-and-loop
fasteners. The problem with most blocks and toy construction kits, writes
McMurray in his patent application, is that "there is normally only one
'proper' way to assemble the individual pieces." The hook-and-loop was
meant to offer more options for the child to pursue their own individual
designs.

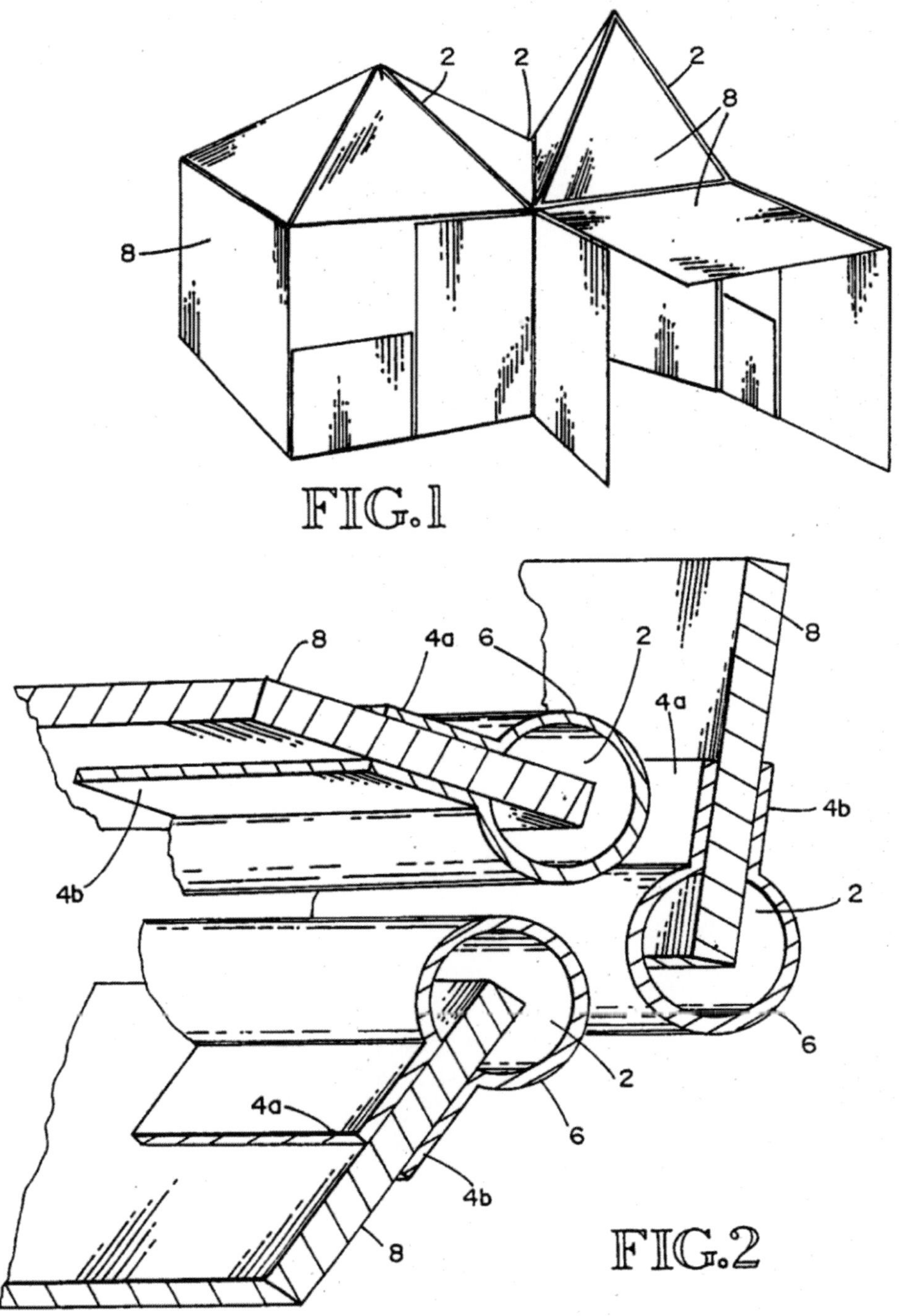

FIG.1

FIG.2

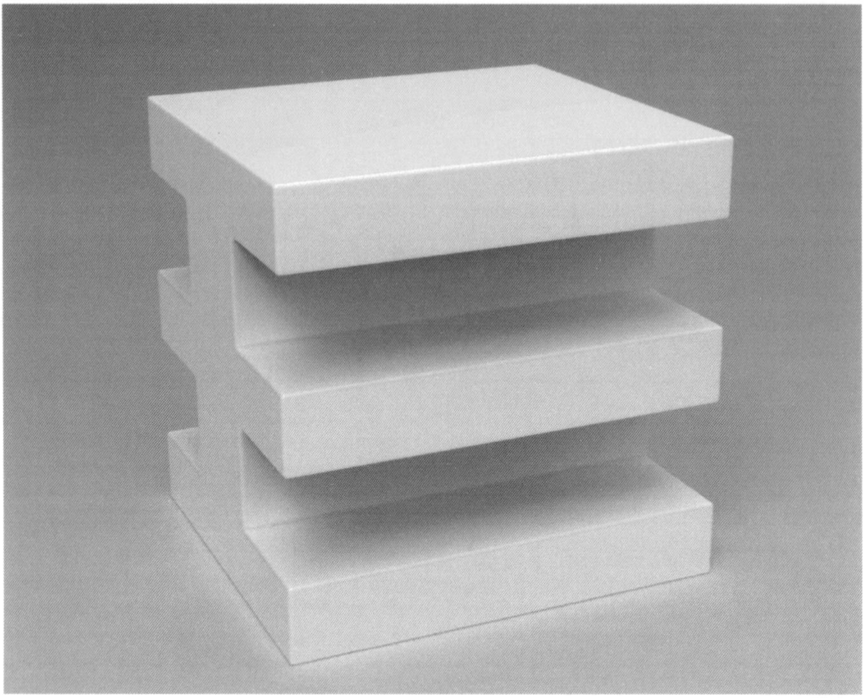

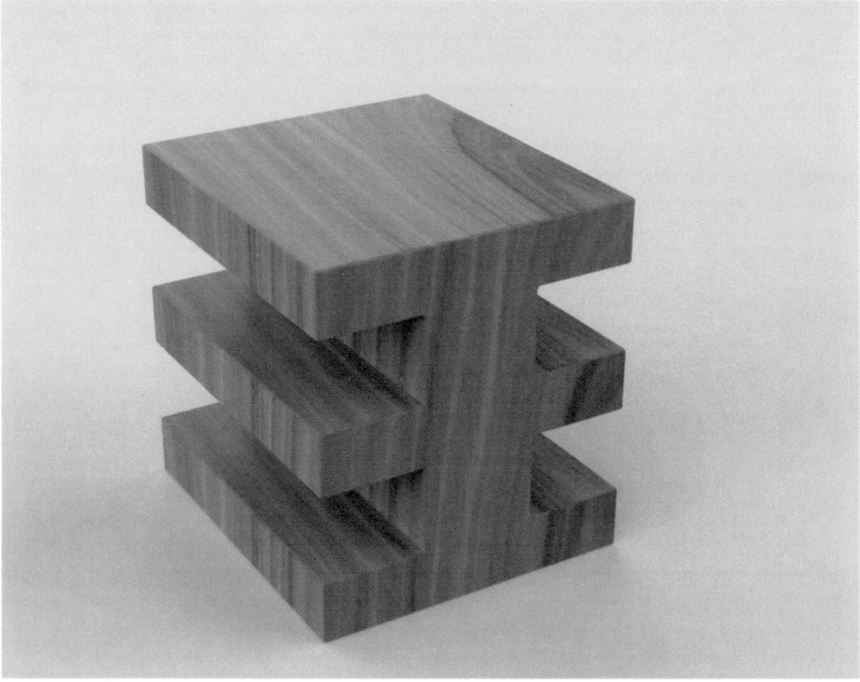

Modular Building Blocks with Interfitted Grooved Surfaces (a.k.a. Picazo blocks)

United States Patent 3,660,928
Inventor: Jorge Picazo Michel, Mexico City, Mexico
Filed Auugst 28, 1970, granted May 9, 1972

Michel was a Cuban filmmaker who immigrated to Mexico following the 1959 revolution. While living in Mexico City with his large immediate family, he developed his Picazo blocks in the early 1970s. Sets were to consist of several pieces of the five basic types pictured below, which could be combined into any number of architectural shapes. He registered a copyright for the invention in 1971, and the patent was granted in 1972. It's unclear if Picazo blocks were ever widely manufactured or distributed in the United States, though a Spanish-language memoir by Michel's daughter, Tessie Gutiérrez de Picazo, notes that a contemporary magazine profile of him once mentioned approvingly that Picazo blocks were "worthy of constructing Kublai Khan's palace at Xanadu."

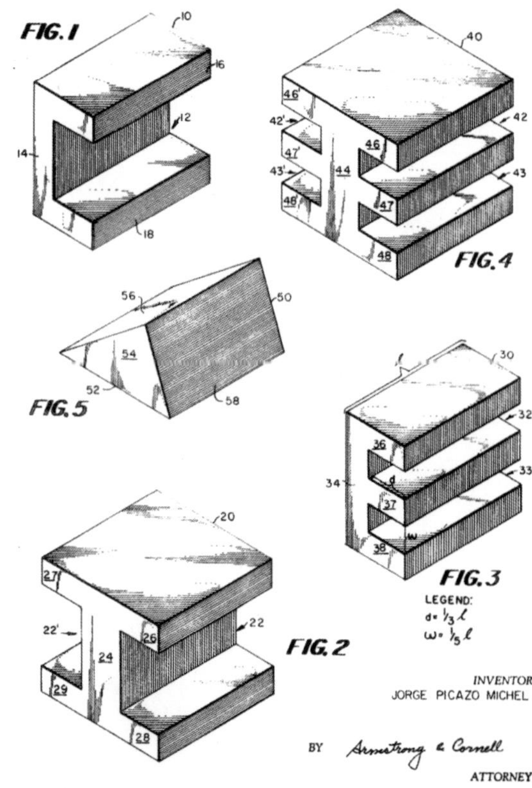

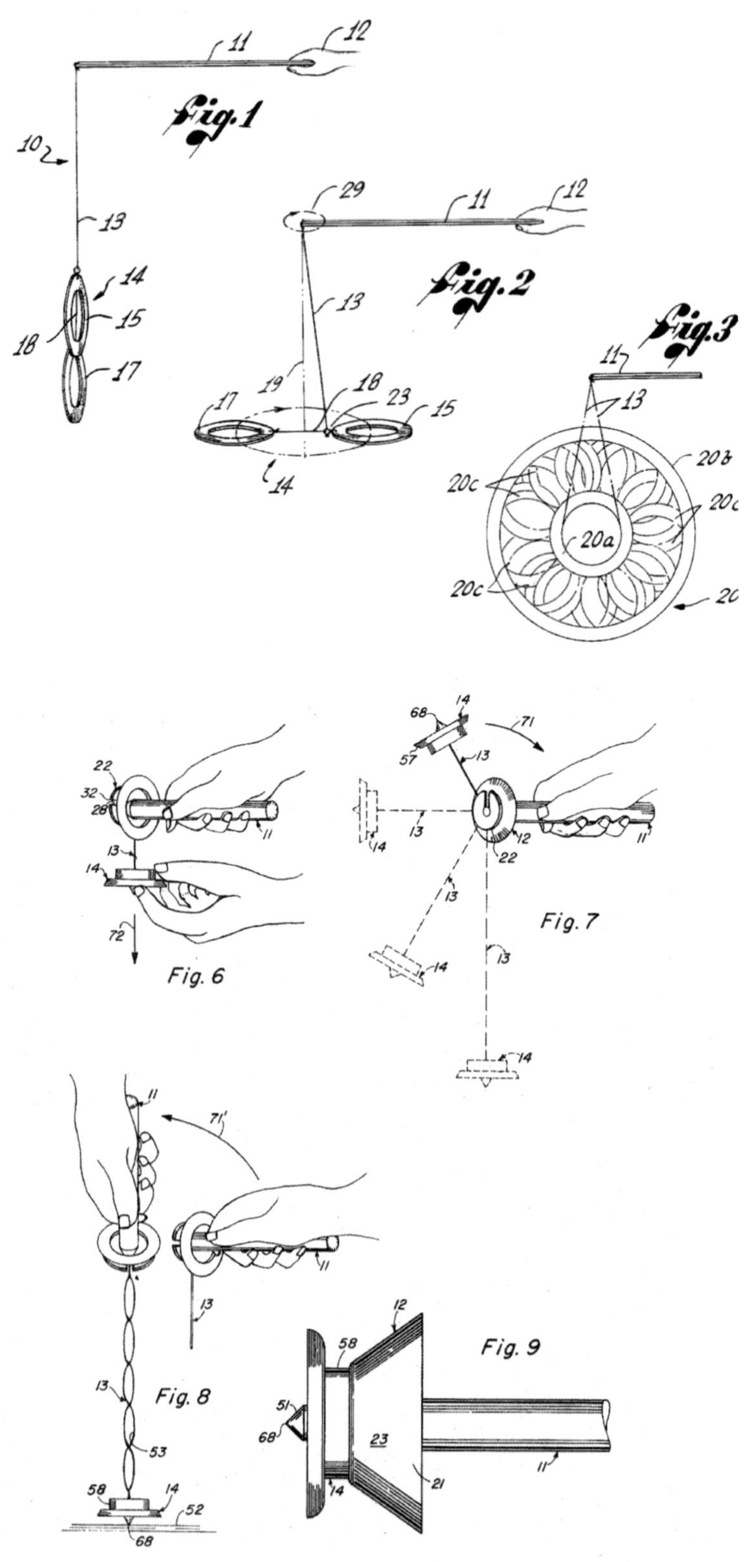

Fig.1
11
12
10
13
14
15
18
17

29
11
12
Fig.2
13
19
17
18
23
15
14

Fig.3
11
13
20b
20c
20c
20a
20c
20

22
32
28
13
14
11
72
Fig. 6

68
14
71
57
13
13
22
12
14
13
14
13
14
Fig. 7

11
71
13
13
53
58
14
52
68
Fig. 8

12
58
51
68
23
14
21
11
Fig. 9

TOP: Whirling Toy
United States Patent 3,940,878
Inventor: Daniel Panico, Santa Monica, Calif.
Filed August 19, 1974, granted March 2, 1976

**BOTTOM: Rotatable Bobbin and Tethered
Spinning Object**
United States Patent: 3,858,348
Inventor: Paul L. Brown, Redwood, Calif.
Filed November 19, 1973, granted January 7, 1975

Both of these whirling and spinning toys, designed by
two Southern Californians, build on the resurgence of
interest in yo-yos that began in the 1960s. Yo-yos created the possibility of all sorts of imaginative spinning
tricks, and both of these designs sought to improve
on the relatively simple yo-yo with a more complex
device. Paul Brown's description of his spinning toy is
a catalog of enhanced tricks familiar to yo-yo enthu-
siasts: jumping the fence, whip action, figure 8s, over
the rainbow, rock-a-bye baby, and "deep sleep while
spinning," a basic yo-yo trick that involves spinning
the yo-yo at the end of its tether. Panico's description of his invention does much the same, though he
sprinkles his with perhaps a dusting of mysticism. The
problem with most of these types of toys, he writes,
is the "limited variety of permissable activity" and
the "absence of any intrigue or mystery in the effects
that could be achieved." Mastery of his toy, he writes,
offers not only a progressively challenging set of skills
to master, but also retains "a degree of mystery or
intrigue in its operation." It calls to mind nothing if not
a very 1970s-appropriate vision of a generation of
neighborhood grade-school spinning monks, dazzling
their peers with displays of inexplicable skill on this
strange device.

Ball and Raceway Amusement Device

United States Patent 3,702,901
Inventor: Tadas Zilius, Hopewell, N.J.; and Joseph
Simboli, Cheyney, Pa.
Filed February 25, 1971, granted November 7, 1972

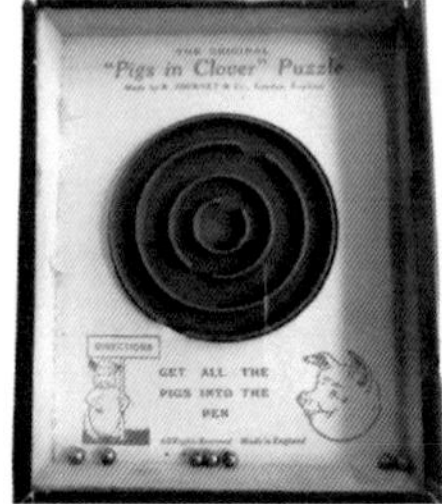

Another patent for Creative Playthings, this is a
more open-ended version of much older games like
"Tree the Possum" or "Pigs in Clover" (left). In these
handheld game devices, popular since the early 20th
century, the player tilts the toy to roll a marble up or
down a grooved labyrinth to the center of an enclosed
box. Later versions of this game enclosed the track in
a transparent plastic, making it impossible to lose the
marble. Zilius and Simboli sought to improve upon
this in two ways: first, in this two-sided design, the ball
is not contained within a box or enclosure, mean-
ing it can be played on the concave side by younger
children, as well as the more advanced convex side
by older children. Secondly, the fact that the ball is
free-rolling improves upon the earlier versions, which
"lack a certain challenge" and in which there "is no
risk." While a lip on the sides prevents the ball from
falling out of the device completely, it does require
a higher degree of dexterity to guide the ball to the
center, especially using the convex side. That idea of
"risk" is one you encounter in many of these designs –
the lack of boundaries, roles, or proscription is meant
to encourage creativity and freer play.

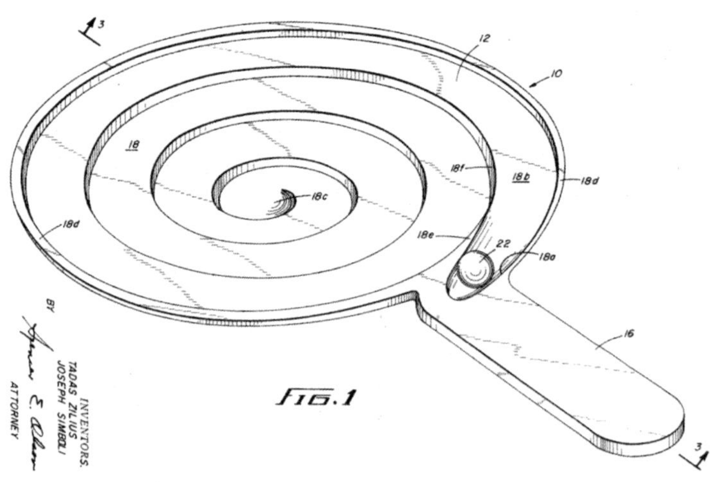

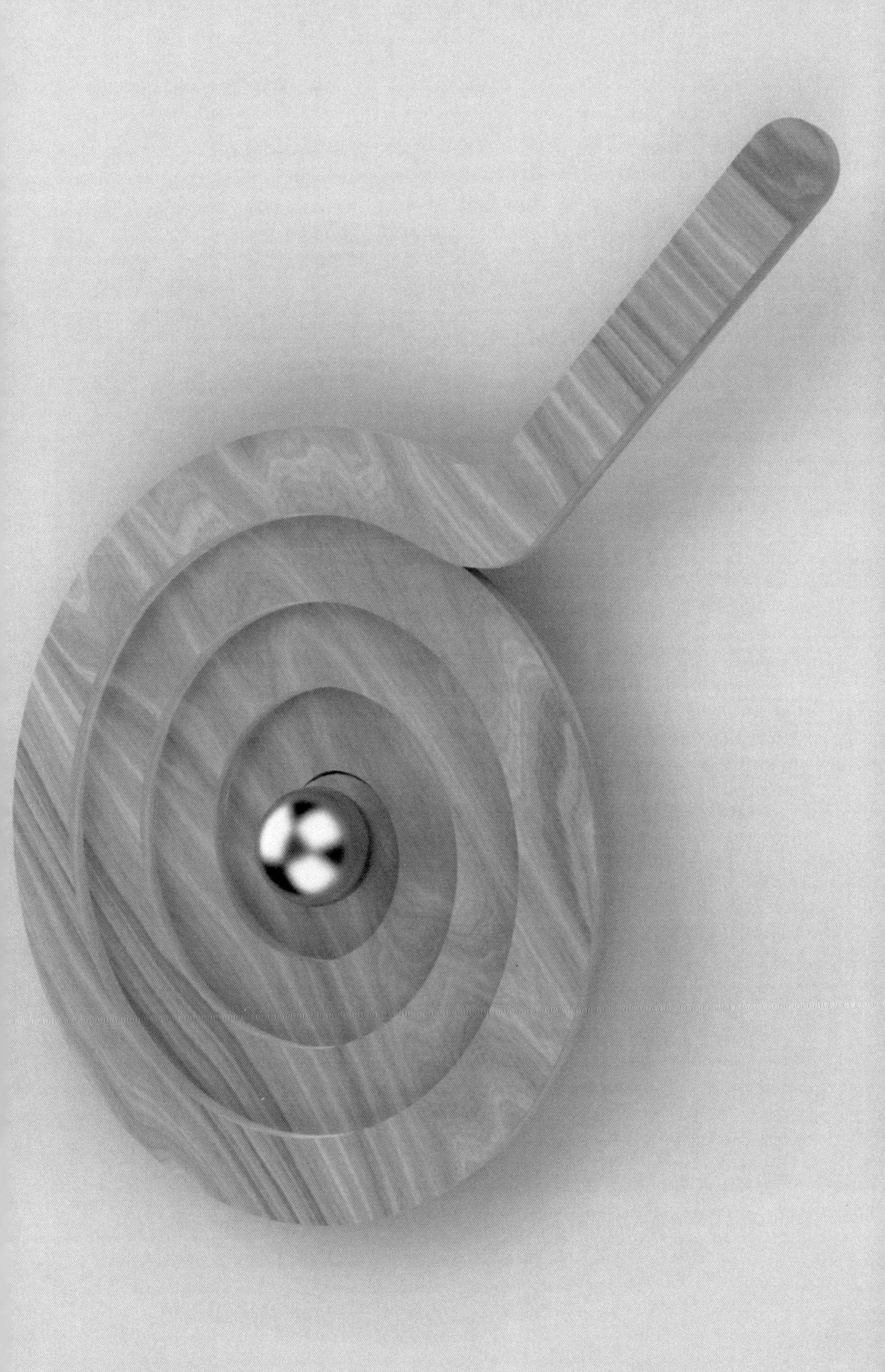

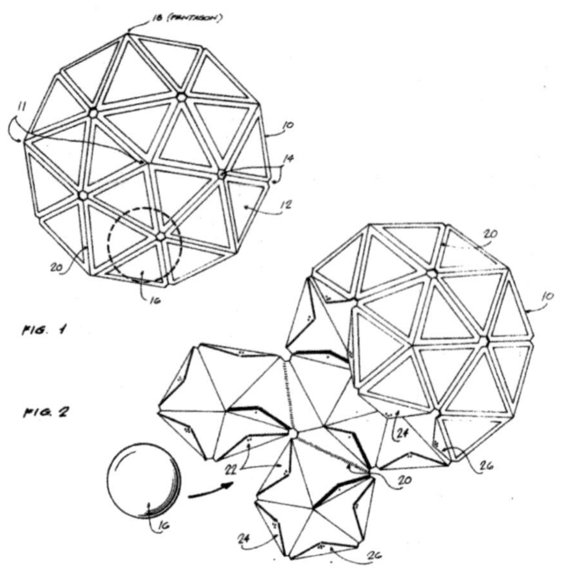

TOP: Polyhedrons Having Depressible Vertices and Internal Means for Restoring Shape
United States Patent 3,605,324
Inventor: Wilbur Henry Adams, New York City, N.Y.
Filed March 7, 1968, granted September 20, 1971

RIGHT: Puzzle Employing Movable Member in Tubular Maze
United States Patent 3,989,255
Inventor: Jerry Raffa, Healdsburg, Calif.
Filed October 21, 1975, granted November 2, 1976

Raffa's mind-bending puzzle involved moving a brightly colored red bean through a jumbled maze of clear plastic tubing to a removable central cup, a more psychedelic, Plastic Age version of the sort of "ball and raceway" toy found on the preceding page. The patent was filed through the Raymond Lee Organization, a group that assisted inventors with their patent ideas. It's not known if Raffa's experience with the Lee Organization was a good one, but it likely was not: the organization faced a variety of lawsuits in the late '70s from the Federal Trade Commission, alleging that the company had defrauded "thousands of customers" lured in by deceptive advertising, charging them exorbitant fees for patent filings "then delivering practically nothing," according to a 1977 *New York Times* article.

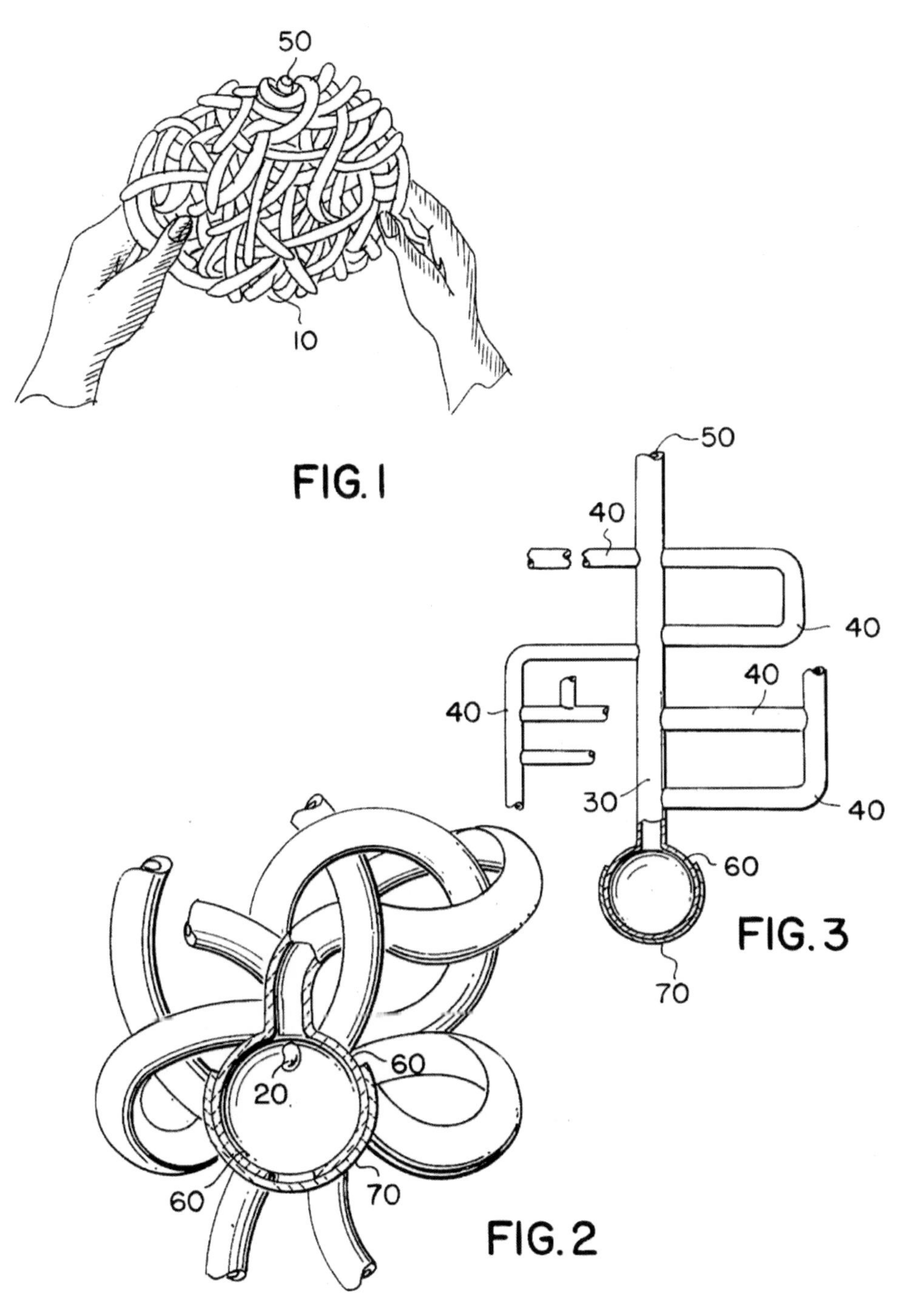

50
10
FIG.1
50
40
40
40
40
40
30
60
70
FIG.3
60
20
60
70
FIG.2

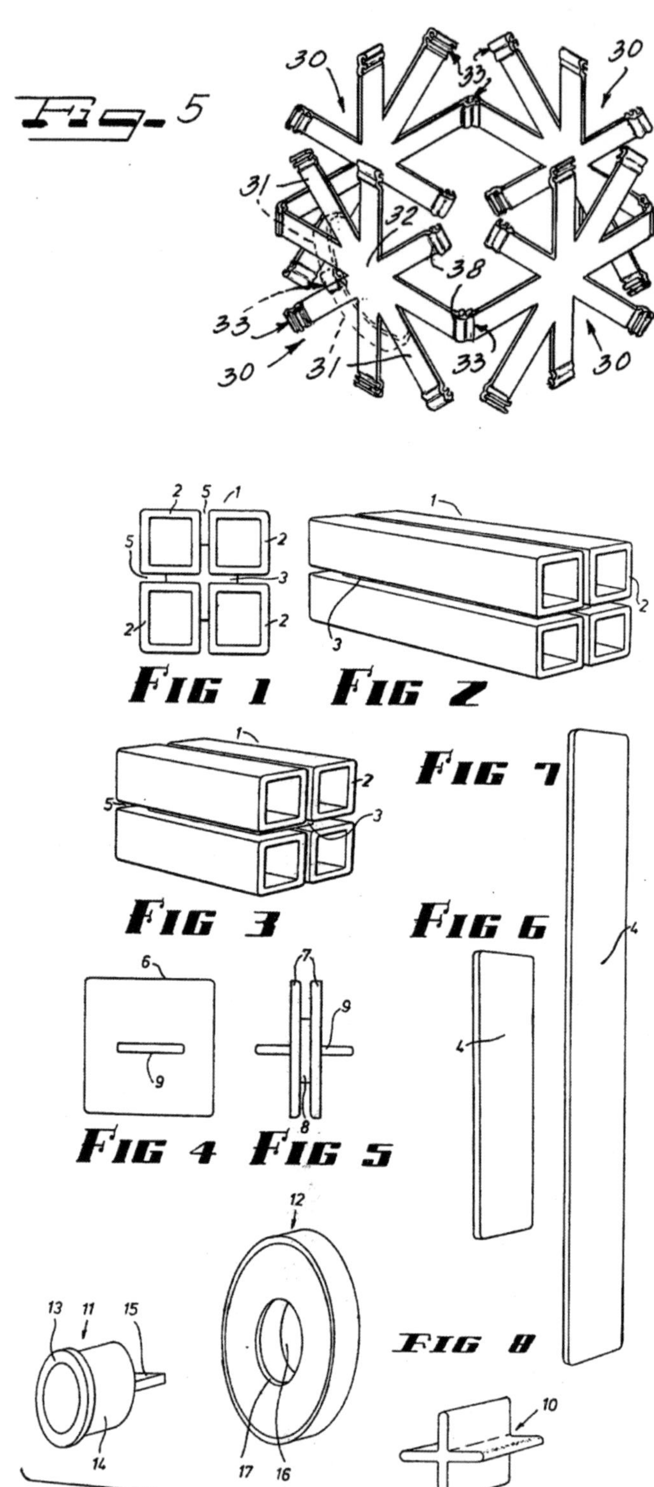

Fig-5
30
33
30
31
32
38
33
30
31
33
30
2
5
1
2
5
2
3
2
2
FIG 1
1
2
3
2
FIG 2
1
2
5
3
FIG 3
FIG 7
FIG 6
4
6
9
7
9
8
4
FIG 4
FIG 5
12
13 11 15
14
17 16
FIG 8
10
FIG 9

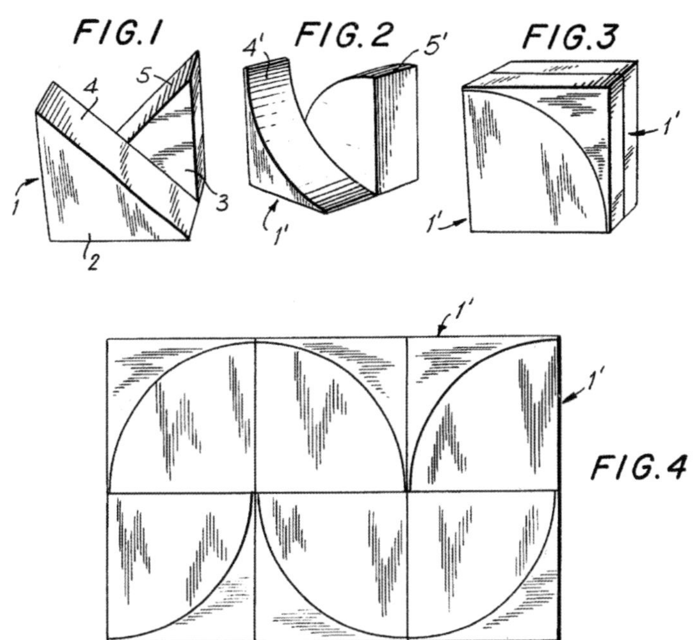

TOP LEFT: Separably Connective Flexible Toy
United States Patent 3,987,580
Inventor: Steve Ausnit, New York City, N.Y.
Filed July 17, 1975, granted October 26, 1976

BOTTOM LEFT: Educational Toy
United States Patent 4,143,481
Inventor: Stephen J. Loechel, Klemzig, Australia
Filed December 15, 1976, granted March 13, 1979

ABOVE: Sectional Toy Blocks
United States Patent 4,011,683
Inventor: Emilio José Jordao De Sousa, Lisbon, Portugal
Filed Auugst 21, 1975, granted September 15, 1977

These are three designs in which "various elements co-operate to fit
together to form a desired structure," as Stephen J. Loechel of Australia
writes in his patent application. The building block is perhaps the oldest
type of plaything, so improvements upon it had better bring something
new to the table. At times, these types of efforts to differentiate their own
creations from two centuries of tradition could be read as a bit hyperbolic:
in his application for these admittedly brilliant sectional toy blocks, Emilio
José Jordao De Sousa claims that "heretofore, no shape has been known
which when associated with others allows a practically unlimited number of
compositions that can be used as pedagogic means."

Stacking Toy with Inner and Outer Stacking Components

United States Patent 3,765,121
Inventor: Jorma Vennola, Princeton, N.J.
Filed February 22, 1972, granted October 16, 1973

Another Vennola design for Creative Playthings, this design seems to foreshadow his career as a maker of high-end, visually sophisticated sculptural objects. This toy was meant to provide a more engaging alternative to the sort of plastic ring-stacking toys that were (and remain) an ubiquitous feature of children's toy chests – toys which, in Vennola's words, "do not require particularly subtle interaction of fitted parts." Though it's a simple design, the various parts can be assembled and disassembled by a very young child in, yes, a relatively subtle way. In its assembled state, though, it works well (perhaps even better) as the sort of interesting, abstract art object you might find on the coffee tables of more aesthetically discerning parents of the era.

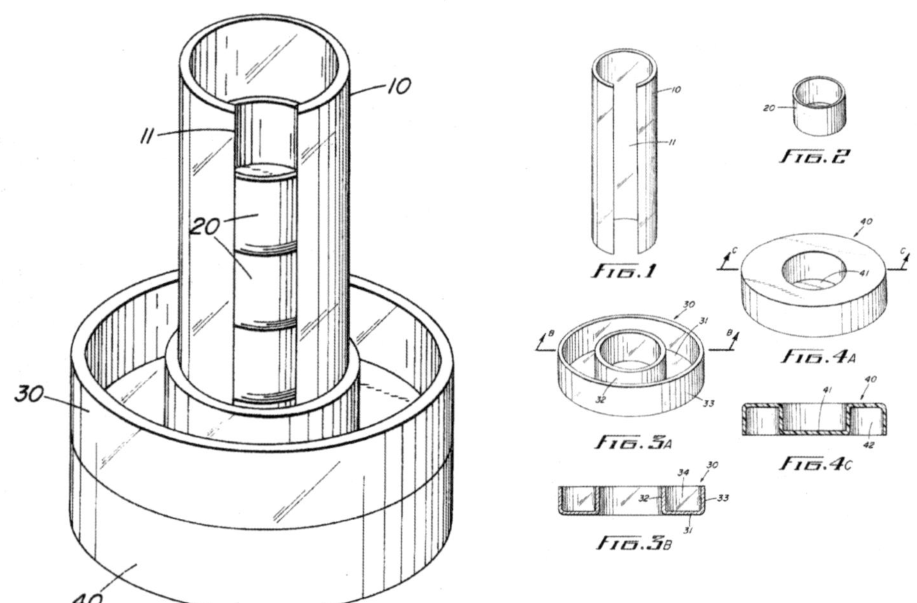

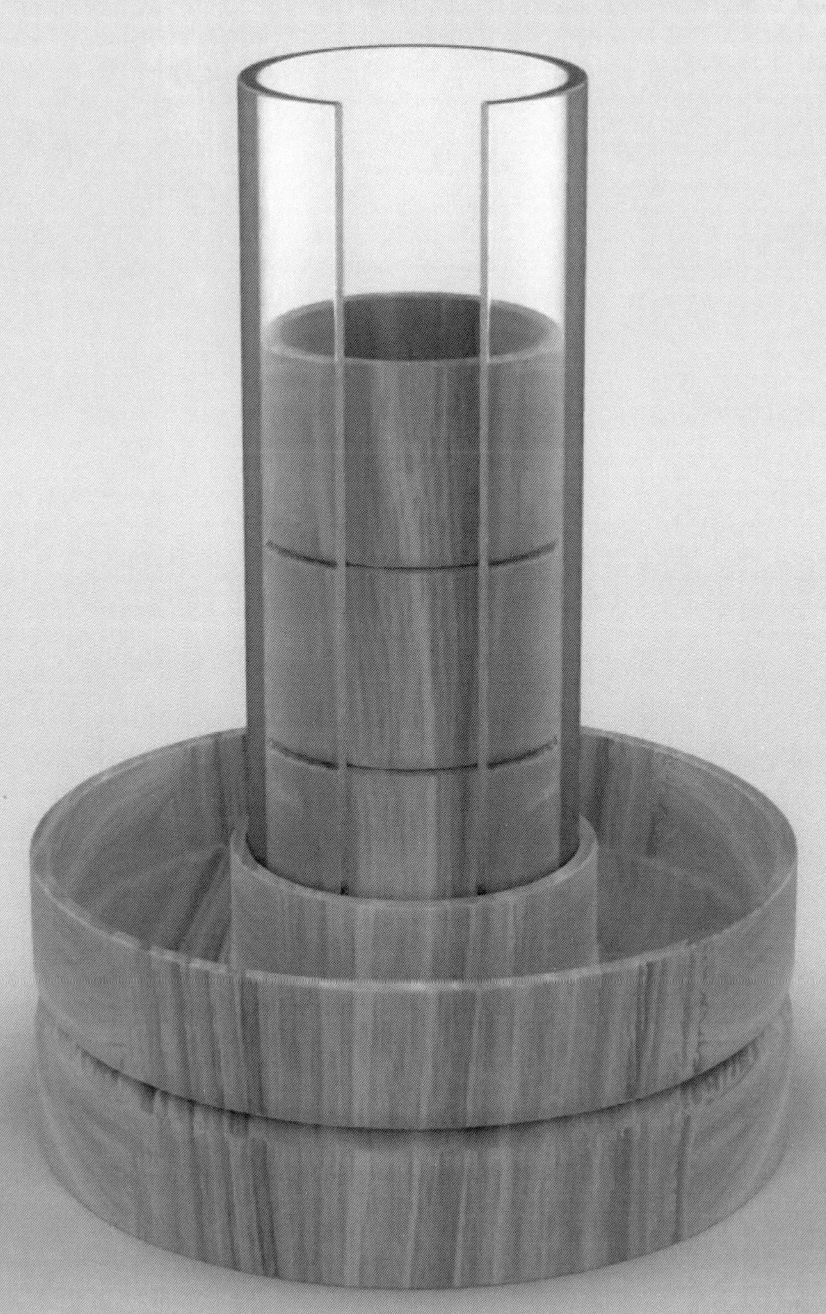

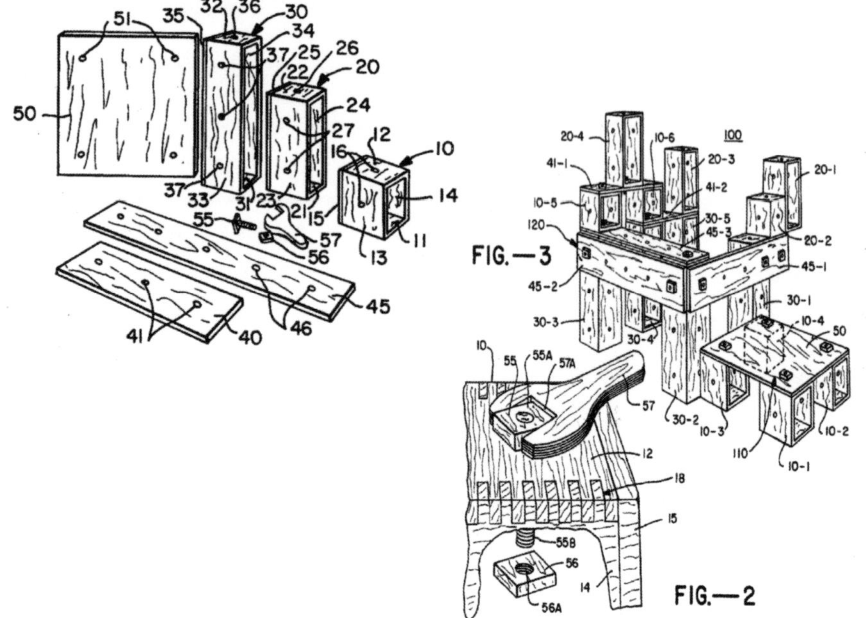

ABOVE: Bolt-Together Building Set for Children

United States Patent 4,389,808
Inventor: Jack Podell and Douglas Haner, San Francisco, Calif.
Filed June 1, 1981, granted June 28, 1983

RIGHT: Log-Splitting Toy

United States Patent 4,834,687
Inventor: Ronald J. Elam, Oakland, Ill.
Filed July 7, 1987, granted May 30, 1989

The best parts about many of the designs collected in this book is how forward-thinking they are, how they fully embrace modernity, and reject sentimental notions of childhood nostalgia. However, there are a few designs included in this book that incorporate traditional tools to create play experiences that mimic workaday tasks that children might find themselves doing on weekends in another ten or fifteen years, like tightening the legs on an endtable with a wrench out in the garage. Ronald J. Elam's plastic firewood-splitting simulator in particular is an inadvertedly hilarious literal recreation of an activity that only a decade or two earlier, plenty of rural and/or back-to-the-land dads were still making their kids go outside to do regularly.

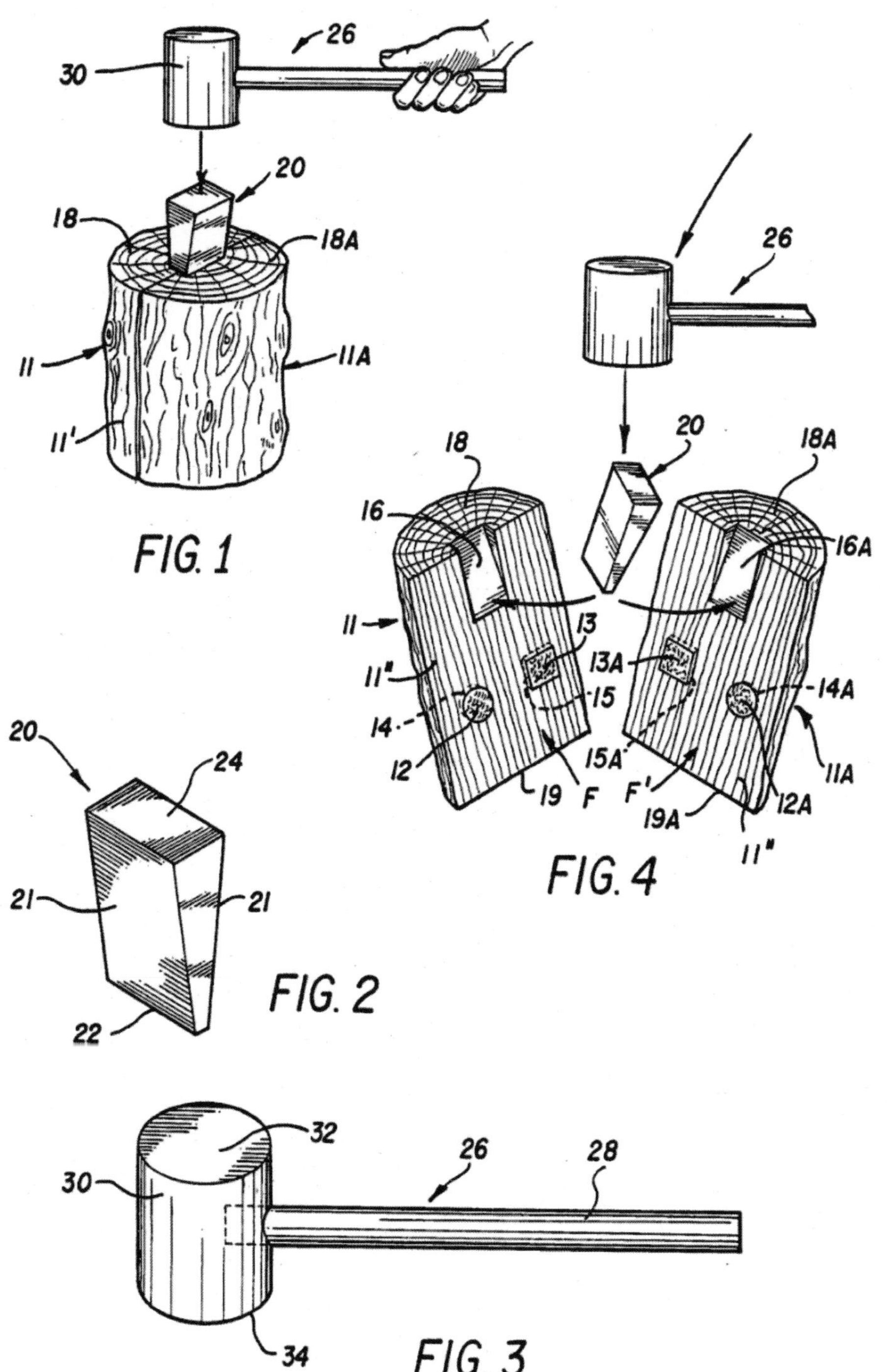

30
26
20
18
18A
11
11'
11A
FIG. 1
20
24
21
21
22
FIG. 2
26
20
18
16
18A
16A
11
13
13A
11"
14
13A
15
14
14A
12
15A
F
F'
12A
19
F
19A
11A
11"
12A
FIG. 4
30
32
26
28
34
FIG. 3

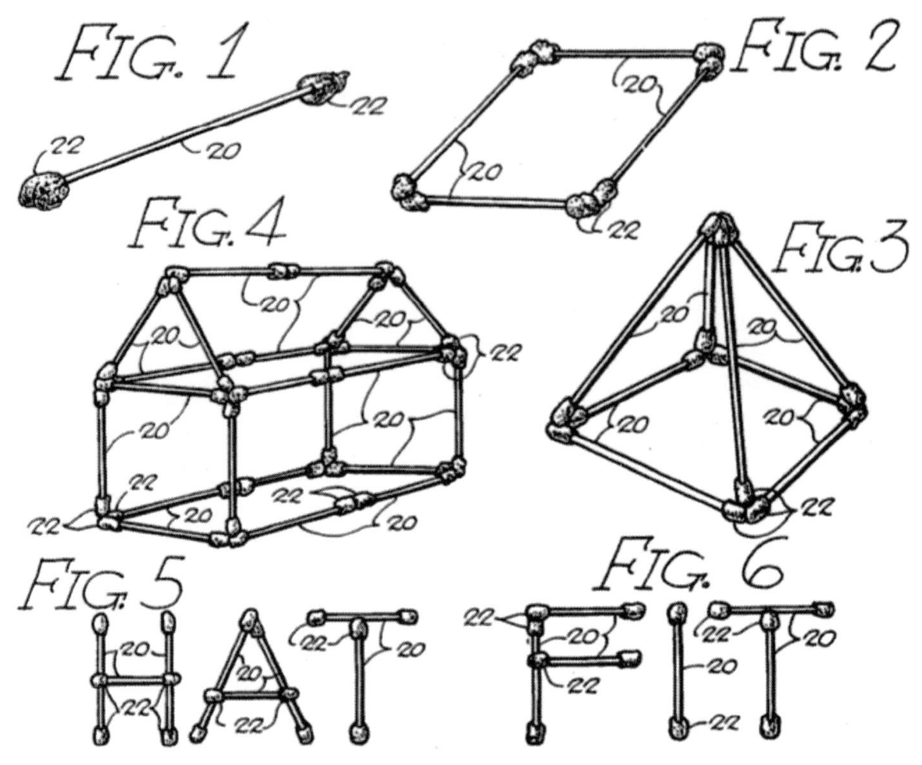

Self-Adhering Sticks, Plates and Other Educational Devices for Constructing Letters, Figures, Designs and the Like

United States Patent 4,259,790
Inventor: Bernard Borisof, Chicago, Ill.
Filed March 4, 1977, granted April 7, 1981

Dowel rods, matchsticks, and other wooden sticks have a long and storied history as playthings, used in everything from simpler games like jackstraws to the strategy game Nim. Chicago architectural engineer Bernard Borisof's design updates the idea for the Plastic Age. Resembling Q-tips, these polypropelene sticks would have a tacky, pressure-sensitive glob of adhesive on each end, made from microcrystaline wax with mineral oil "in the proportion of 2 to 12% mixed with the wax," along with a small amount of low molecular weight polyethelene. The sticks could be joined at the ends or temporarily adhered to flat surfaces to make designs or drawings. Borisof imagined the toys being used not only by children, but by the blind as a tactile educational aid.

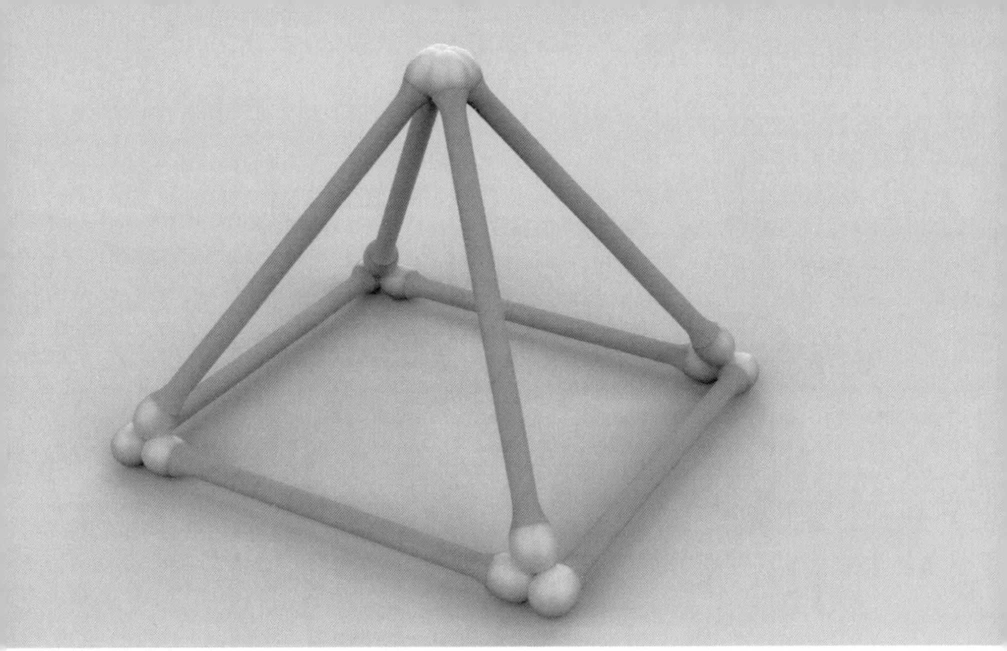

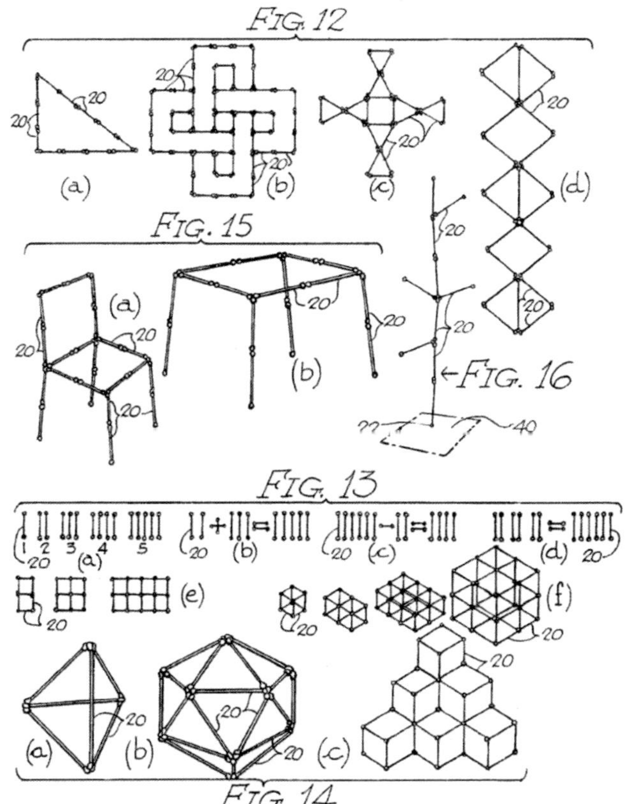

FIG. 12
20
20
20
20
(a)
(b)
(c)
(d)
FIG. 15
20
20
(a)
20
20
20
(b)
20
20
←FIG. 16
??
40
FIG. 13
1 2 3 4 5
20
(a)
20
(b)
20
(c)
20
(d)
20
(e)
20
(f)
20
20
20
(a)
20
(b)
20
(c)
FIG. 14

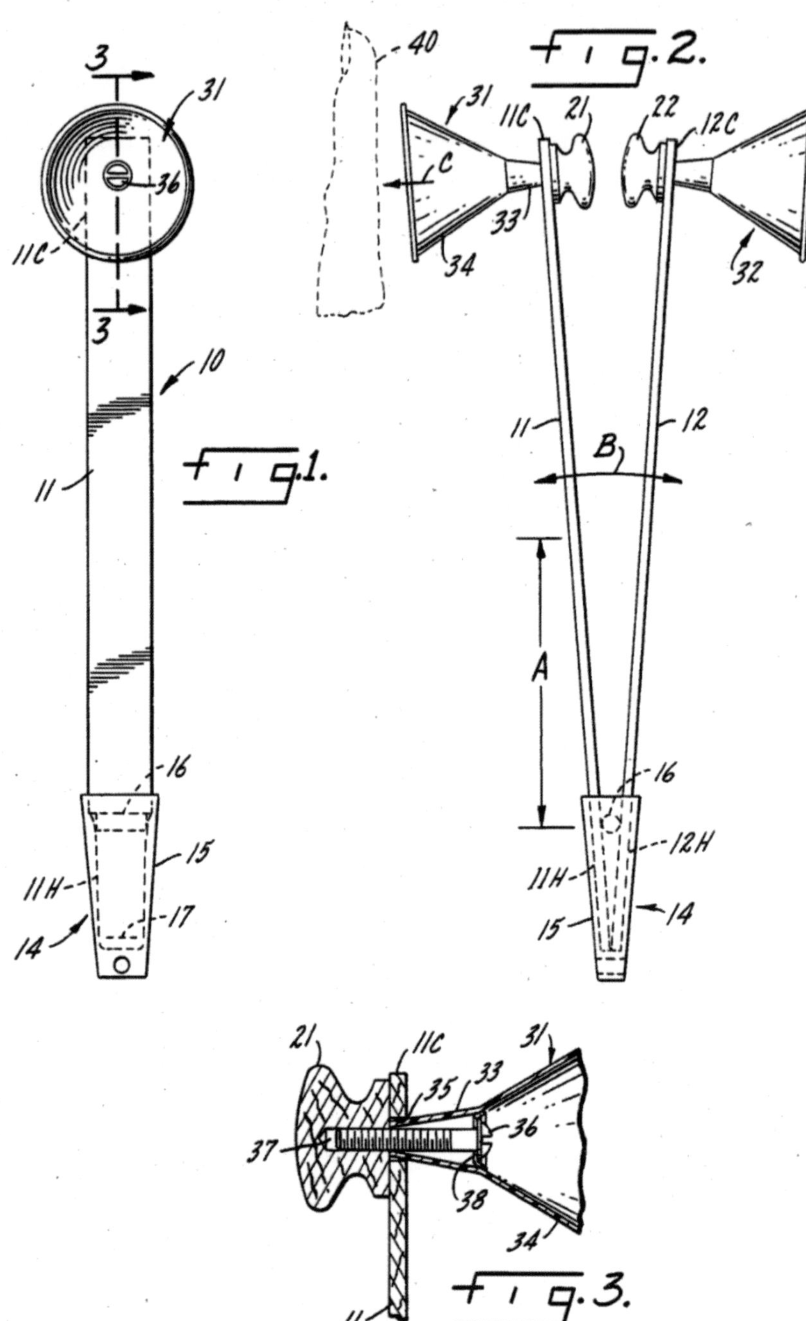

3
31
36
11C
3
10
11
Fig.1.
40
Fig.2.
31
11C
21
22
12C
C
33
34
32
11
12
B
A
16
12H
11H
14
15
16
12H
11H
14
15
21
11C
31
33
35
36
37
38
34
11
Fig.3.

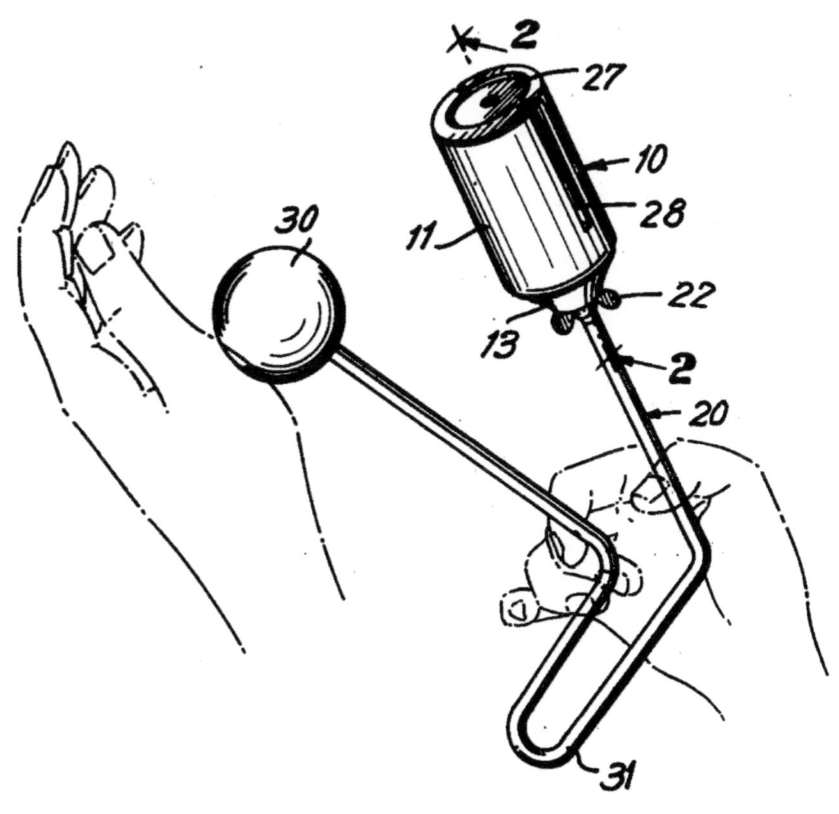

LEFT: Percussion Noisemaker
United States Patent 4,658,694
Inventor: Lawrence Marks, Chicago, Ill.
Filed August 26, 1985, granted April 21, 1987

ABOVE: Percussion Instrument
United States Patent 4,127,053
Inventor: Martin Cohen, Maywood, N.J.
Filed June 17, 1977, granted November 28, 1978

Toy Block Having Paneled Construction (a.k.a. "Star Blocks")

United States Patent 3,787,996
Inventors: John A. Smith, Mercerville, N.J. and
Stephen A. Miller, New York City, N.Y.
Filed August 15, 1972, granted January 28, 1974

Another patent for Creative Playthings during the CBS era, these so called "star blocks" were co-developed by Creative Playthings president Stephen A. Miller. Miller was a colorful figure who, previous to his tenure at CBS, had ran a boutique toy store in Greenwich Village where famed artist Joseph Cornell was said to have bought the boxes he used in his assemblages.

The blocks were trademarked and sold under the name Naefspiele, or "Naef Games," under an agreement with German toy manufacturer Naef. Kurt Naef (1926-2006) developed the originals for his Naef Company in 1954. Sold in sets of sixteen, these original blocks were made of wood. This patent proposes to manufacture them from plastic that would be injection-molded into a single-cavity mold. This process would make them lightweight and, to the minds of the inventors, less expensive, more durable, and lacking the risk of "toxic" paints potentially found it their wood counterparts. Incidentally, the Naef Company still sells hand-crafted star blocks today which, like the originals, are handcrafted from wood.

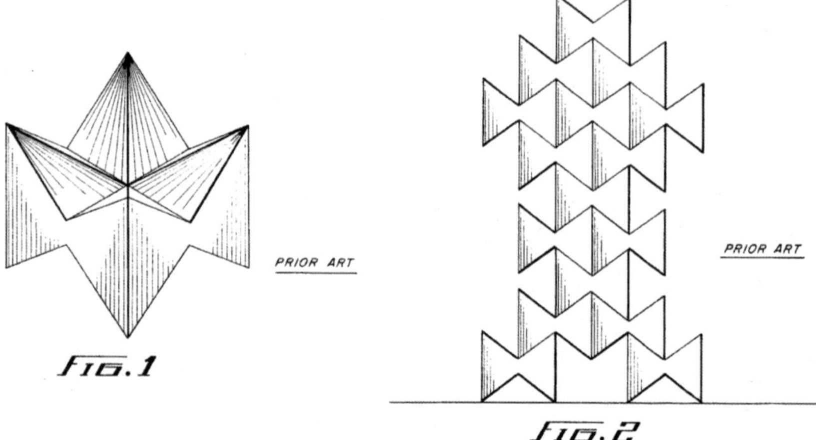

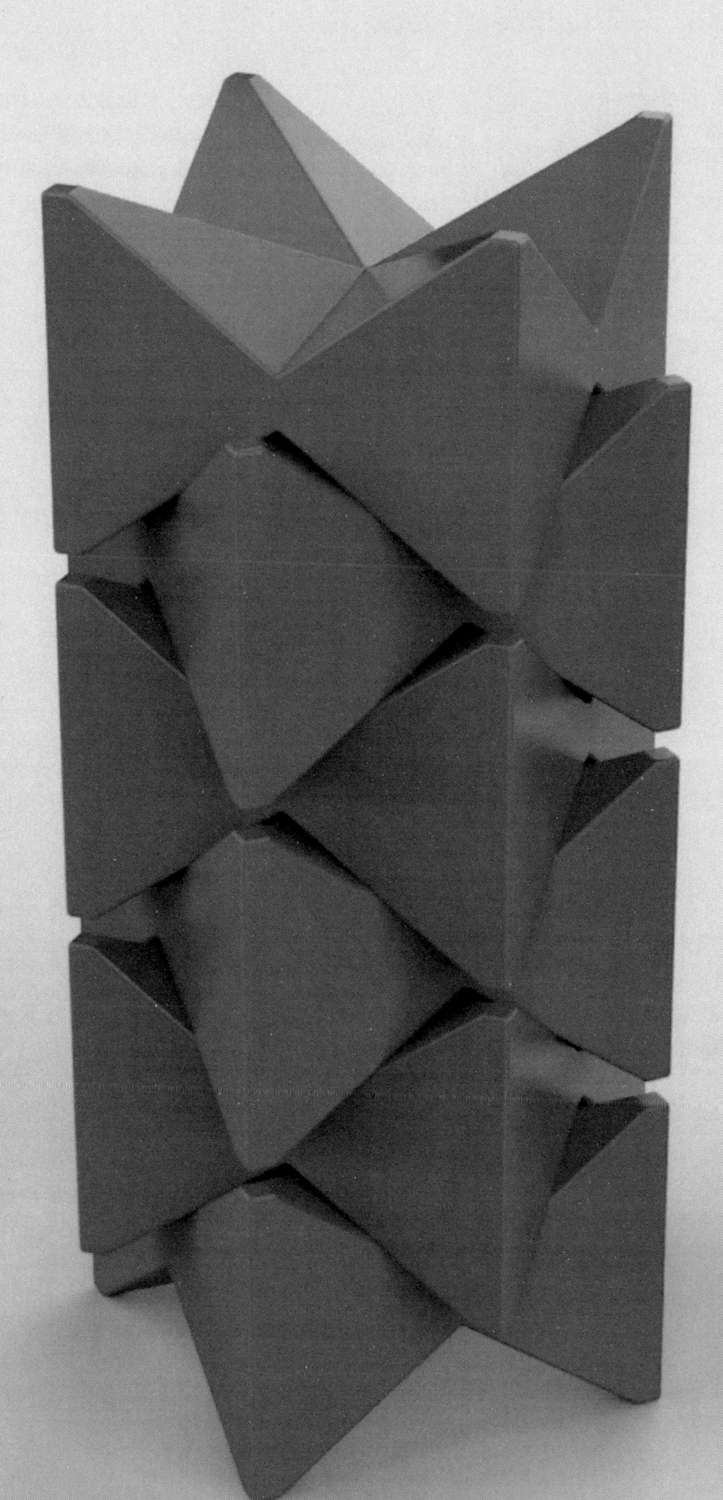

A note on the illustrations

Most of the designs in this book, if not all, never made it to market. As evocative as the patent drawings are as both art objects and guides to visualizing the toys, I commissioned two digital arts studios, **Three D Studios** and **Aeriveros Studios**, to digitally render photorealistic images of some of the best designs, pictured in this book to resemble period-appropriate black-and-white product photographs. It gives them a chance to exist in something a little bit closer to a corporeal state.

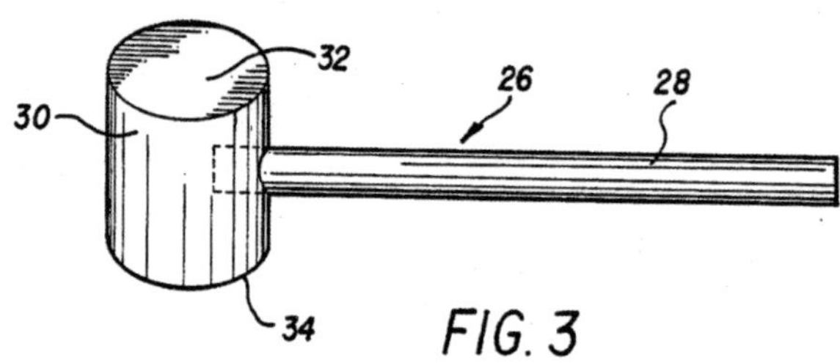

Dedicated to my grandmother, Flora Dickerson Lawyer (1919-1988), employee of Kenner Toys, Cincinnati; and to my mother, Nancy Ann Lawyer Sturdevant, a lifelong children's art educator who has always disliked plastic war toys.

Patent research assistance by Jacque Annette, Esq., Miami, Fl.

Editorial assistance by Cassandra Chloe Sison, New York City, N.Y., and Jillian Keener Marinovic, New Orleans, La.

Printed in Carver County, Minnesota, the traditional and contemporary homelands of the Sisseton and Wahpeton bands of the Dakhóta people. A percentage of Birchwood Palace Industries' annual revenue is contributed to Dakota Wicohan, a Native-led non-profit educational organization located within the Lower Sioux Indian Community that seeks to revitalize the Dakota language and lifeways in Minnesota. Learn more about the organization at dakotawicohan.org.